W9-DDJ-437

WITHDRAWN

THE CALL OF DUTY
CAREERS IN THE
ARMED FORCES™

YOUR CAREER IN

THE MARINES

COLLEEN RYCKERT COOK

ROSEN
PUBLISHING®

New York

To the men and women of the United States Marine Corps

Published in 2012 by The Rosen Publishing Group, Inc.
29 East 21st Street, New York, NY 10010

Copyright © 2012 by The Rosen Publishing Group, Inc.

First Edition

Library of Congress Cataloging-in-Publication Data

Cook, Colleen Ryckert.
Your career in the marines/Colleen Ryckert Cook.
 p. cm.—(The call of duty: careers in the armed forces)
Includes bibliographical references and index.
ISBN 978-1-4488-5512-4 (library binding)
1. United States. Marine Corps—Juvenile literature.
2. United States. Marine Corps—Vocational guidance—
Juvenile literature. I. Title.
VE23.C737 2012
359.9'602373—dc22

                                        2011008648

Manufactured in the United States of America

CPSIA Compliance Information: Batch #W12YA: For further information, contact Rosen Publishing, New York, New York, at 1-800-237-9932.

CONTENTS

Introduction...4

Chapter 1: Do You Have What It Takes?...8

Chapter 2: Learning the Basics...18

Chapter 3: Combat Specialties...33

Chapter 4: Vehicle/Machinery
and Mechanics...42

Chapter 5: Electronic/Electrical Systems...51

Chapter 6: Personnel and Base Support...66

Chapter 7: Logistics and Supply...79

Chapter 8: Engineering, Science,
and Technical...89

Chapter 9: Life After the Military...100

Glossary...112
For More Information...114
For Further Reading...118
Bibliography...121
Index...124

INTRODUCTION

So you want to be a United States Marine. Here's a glimpse of one day in the life of four different marines around the world:

Cobra Gold jungle training, Chon Buri Province, Thailand: The marine sits among the dense foliage, his heavy boots covered in red mud, and eyes a scorpion warily. Its body is big enough to nearly fill the marine's hand. With a lightning strike he grasps the dangerous tail, kills the insect, and pops it into his mouth. His fellow marines cheer. This isn't a stunt that would make Johnny Knoxville proud. It is survival at its most basic. You must learn how to feed yourself, protect yourself, and move about in all climates. If you can't find food and water when you're in the field with limited supplies, you won't come out of the jungle alive. And scorpions are packed with protein.

Marine Corps Mountain Warfare Training Center, Bridgeport, California: The small marine team dug out the shallow snow trenches the night before, after climbing 6 miles (10 kilometers) by moonlight in up to 3 feet (1 meter) of snow in some places. You can't find them at first. A marine instructor must point

A U.S. Marines firing detail stands in silent attention as they recall the lives lost during a memorial service for the sixty-ninth anniversary of the attack on the U.S. Naval base at Pearl Harbor.

them out before you see them. Their white climate suits blend into the snow, and their bark-covered helmets look like exposed twigs and rocks. It took them three hours to move into position on the Sierra Nevada mountaintop 10,000 feet (3,048 m) above sea level. These marines are already highly skilled snipers, but they have been picked for this intensive mountain training course to succeed in the harsh Afghanistan mountains. They will learn to fortify their positions in freezing, rocky mountaintops. They'll learn to shoot at steep angles under the most extreme conditions. There is a mini-stove to melt snow for water. Through binoculars they spot their target, a single shadowy figure in an open doorway 1,000 feet (305 m) below. They don't take the shot. Precision is everything, they say. One shot. One kill. They can wait.

Parris Island, South Carolina: Thirty-two hours into the Crucible. A dozen marines working together as a team have just received their mission: "You have twenty minutes to move all personnel and all equipment from one side of this wall and down the other." The wall is 15 feet (4.6 m) high, smooth wood, with no hand or foot holds. The team springs into action. Within fifteen seconds the strongest of the group has been lifted and is now kneeling on the top of the wall. It's roughly 10 inches (25 centimeters) wide. He balances himself and reaches down as his teammates hoist the next marine up. The two grasp hands, and they're both on top of the wall. The second marine jumps to the ground on the other side. A pack comes next. One marine over, eleven to go. They have a little more than eighteen minutes left.

Sangin, Helmand Province, Afghanistan: The IED, or improvised explosive device, was left next to the perimeter fence of the police station sometime in the night. The ammunition and explosives disposal team surrounds it. They must move precisely and with sureness to disarm the bomb before it detonates and kills them and everyone nearby. This is no training exercise. This longtime Taliban stronghold is the center of the opium trade for the southern part of Afghanistan and one of the fiercest war zones. Within a few months of the marines increasing their presence in Sangin in 2010, they had endured more than four hundred firefights and ambushes and came across even more buried roadside bombs. Another hundred exploded before they could find them, killing and injuring soldiers and civilians who travel along the very same roads. The frequency of the firefights and IEDs have slowed, but they keep coming.

This is the typical workday of a U.S. Marine. Are you ready for it?

CHAPTER 1

DO YOU HAVE WHAT IT TAKES?

You've seen the images of "The Few. The Proud. The Marines." You've heard tales of tenacity and fierce loyalty. You want to push yourself mentally and physically to prove that you are worthy to call yourself a jarhead.

Not so fast.

Marines have a stringent recruitment protocol. You must prove yourself before you're even invited to boot camp. They weed out those they believe won't succeed and focus on the few who embody the Marine Corps' values of honor, courage, and commitment.

Marines are said to be "first in combat" for a reason. They serve at the president's discretion to protect American interests around the world. That means they can be deployed to fight at a hint of threat to America or its citizens, even without a congressional declaration of war. They are first responders in a conflict. They assess the layout of the land and causes of turmoil, then prepare for the other servicemen's arrival. A marine is a rifleman first and foremost, regardless of rank or job title.

Not just anyone can join the Marine Corps. If you want to enlist, you must be between eighteen and twenty-nine years old—or seventeen with a parent's consent. You must be working toward or have earned your high school diploma. You must be an American citizen or meet certain requirements for noncitizens.

You also need physical and mental toughness. It takes just over twelve daunting weeks of training to graduate from recruit to marine. The Marine Corps wants total commitment. Are you willing to give eight years of your life to the marines—at least four years of active service and the remaining years in reserve duty?

If your answer is yes, your first step is to talk to a marine recruiter. Recruiters visit high schools during career days. You can prepare first by getting information from your high school guidance counselor or, if your school has a Naval Junior Reserve Officers' Training Corps (NJROTC) program, the senior naval science instructor.

The recruiter will ask what you want for your future and what you want from the Marine Corps. You'll want to ask lots of questions, too, like what does it take to get through boot camp, what can you expect during your service, what kind of training can you expect after graduating, and more.

The decision to join the marines will take you on a path of discipline, determination, and dedication. You'll learn more about yourself in twelve weeks than you have in twelve years of school.

If you and your recruiter think you have what it takes, you'll start the enlistment process. Make an appointment to visit a recruitment office. When that day arrives, show respect for yourself by dressing and behaving accordingly. This is a job interview for a unique career that requires discipline and drive. Be freshly showered with tidy hair. Leave decorative jewelry and any piercings or earlobe gauges at home. Don't wear clothing that has violent or vulgar images or words. If you think those clothes show off your warrior mentality, you're making the wrong impression. If you're female, make sure your makeup, hairstyle, and clothes are modest, even if your personal style is more carefree or colorful.

You'll need to bring a file's worth of important information to your interview. Your recruiter will want to see:

- Your birth certificate
- Social Security card
- A complete medical history, including current medications
- Your high school diploma or transcripts and any college transcripts you might have
- A list of all the places where you've lived
- Your job history, including addresses and names of supervisors
- Four personal references, including all contact information
- A list of places you've traveled outside of the United States
- A history of any troubles you might have had with police, including minor traffic violations
- Noncitizens must bring their permanent resident number (green card) and the date and port of entry into the United States

10 QUESTIONS TO ASK A
MARINE RECRUITER

1. What makes the Marine Corps different from other armed forces?

2. What kind of person thrives in the Marine Corps?

3. How can the Marine Corps improve my leadership and management skills?

4. What specialties and technical skills can I learn?

5. What educational opportunities are available?

6. What kinds of pay and benefits can I expect?

7. What are the requirements for becoming a marine?

8. What do Marine Corps reservists do?

9. Why did you become a marine?

10. How can I prepare for Marine Corps recruit training?

You'll have a chance to talk in depth about salary and benefits, training opportunities, your chances for deployment overseas, and more. The recruiter will review all your paperwork and write up a preliminary medical report. As soon as you're cleared by a doctor, you'll be sent to your local military processing center (MPC) for a complete physical and Armed Services Vocational Aptitude Battery (ASVAB).

Just as you'd do for a school test, you'll want a good night's sleep and a healthy breakfast before you head out to the MPC. The ASVAB is a series of multiple-choice tests. You'll answer questions about science, math and reasoning, electronics, and mechanical comprehension. As the name implies, the test looks for aptitude, or abilities. It helps the Marine Corps to target your strengths and interests so that they can match you with a potential job path.

Your physical examination will include hearing and vision tests. You'll have a blood chemistry profile and will need to give a urine sample to check for drug or alcohol abuse problems. If you're female, you'll take a pregnancy test.

After the tests, you'll meet with a career classifier to discuss possible careers and training. The two of you will go through the enlistment contract before you sign it.

Precision, teamwork, and unified commitment—that's what it means to train as a U.S. Marine. You and your fellow recruits will learn to move as one, think as one, and fight as one.

And then the moment arrives: you stand before a Marine Corps officer, raise your right hand, and recite the oath:

"I, (your name), do solemnly swear that I will support and defend the Constitution of the United States against all enemies, foreign and domestic; that I will bear true faith and allegiance to the same; and that I will obey the orders of the President of the United States and the orders of the officers appointed over me, according to regulations and the Uniform Code of Military Justice."

You won't ship off to boot camp as soon as you utter the last word of the oath. Even with direct-ship orders, it can take anywhere from two days to two months before your call date arrives. Many enlistees choose the Delayed Entry Program (DEP), which gives them up to a year to report for duty. During this time they will interact with other recruits through family nights, organized sports, and other Marine Corps–sponsored events. The DEP lets them organize financial needs, get into better physical shape, finish school, and manage any family issues before they start their new life. This time also lets future recruits prepare themselves mentally for the rigorous twelve weeks of training.

ENTERING THE MILITARY AS A COMMISSIONED OFFICER

There are a few ways you can become a Marine Corps officer. First, and most important, you must be working toward a four-year degree. You must be between seventeen and twenty-three years old and have earned a minimum combined score of 1,000 on your SAT or a composite score of 22 on your ACT.

Unlike the other armed forces, the Marine Corps doesn't have its own academy. Officer candidates can apply to the Naval Academy in Annapolis, Maryland. If you enroll at a traditional college that offers a NJROTC program, you can apply to be a Marine-Option Midshipman. Finally, you can apply to Officer Candidate School in Quantico, Virginia, after you graduate from college.

The selection process for all of these is incredibly competitive. Few of the many who apply are accepted. Even fewer receive scholarships. Talk to your recruiter about the best course for you.

If you are chosen to be a Marine-Option Midshipman, you'll need to succeed at college. You'll take courses required for your chosen degree, but you'll also need to take courses in naval science, ethics, management, and the history of warfare. Throughout your years at college, you'll participate in summer "cruises" where you'll learn more about life in the marines. You might attend Mountain Warfare Training to learn high-altitude and cold-weather movement and survival skills. During your third year you'll attend Marine Officer Candidates School, where you'll be tested on your leadership skills, academic abilities, and physical fitness. If you successfully complete the NJROTC program, you'll earn the rank Second Lieutenant.

Once you've started down this path, you should begin acting like the marine you will become, even if you opt for the DEP. Remove any earlobe gauges and body piercings, even the ones you think nobody will ever see. You can't have them during boot camp training. Do not get a new tattoo. If you're female, consider cutting your hair into a short wash-and-go style that ends above the collar. If you want to keep your long hair, you must be able to pull all of it into a tight bun at the base of your neck.

Hold your appearance and actions to the strictest standards. When you arrive at your Marine Corp recruit base for training, you'll already look the part.

CHAPTER 2

LEARNING THE BASICS

Marine Corps basic training has the reputation of being the toughest of all armed services. It's no exaggeration. It takes just over twelve weeks to go from recruit to marine. In those days you will push yourself harder and further than you ever thought possible.

There are only two places in the United States where enlisted recruits train to become marines: Marine Corps Recruit Depot (MCRD) San Diego in San Diego, California, and MCRD Parris Island in Beaufort, South Carolina. All female recruits and males who live east of the Mississippi River travel to South Carolina, while males who live west of the Mississippi train in San Diego.

YOUR FIRST DAYS

The first few days at the depot are spent in processing. You'll get your gear and platoon assignment. If

Within hours of arriving at the Marine Corps Recruit Depot, recruits find themselves lining up to receive the distinct high and tight buzz haircut. This is the first step to becoming a marine.

you're male, you'll get the mandatory buzz cut. If you need glasses or contacts to correct your vision, you'll get military-issued black plastic frames that you must wear throughout boot camp instead. A doctor will give you a complete physical.

You'll also take and must pass the Initial Strength Test (IST). The IST is made up of three different skills. You'll take the test in one day within a two-hour period. At minimum, all males must be able to complete two hanging pull-ups, forty-four crunches in two

GETTING TO GUNG HO

To become a marine, you must first relinquish your individuality. You'll find this out when you meet your drill instructors. During boot camp your name is "recruit," and on day one they'll start dismantling your ego so that you can be remolded into a marine.

The first lesson you learn is to not use personal pronouns, such as "I," "me," or "my" when referring to yourself, or "he," "she," or "they" when talking about fellow recruits. You must refer to yourself as "this recruit" and the others as "that recruit" or "those recruits." When speaking to a drill instructor, you must say "the drill instructor" instead of "you."

It's this stripping away of self that makes marines a force of one, the gung-ho spirit that epitomizes the marine experience. *Gung ho* is a Chinese term that means "to work in harmony."

Brigadier General Evans F. Carlson, USMCR, first heard the term while in northern China in 1937. When he later became commander of the 2nd Marine Raider Battalion, a group trained for raiding and guerilla missions, he knew he wanted men who embodied that sense of unified commitment. In his words:

"Gung Ho! To Work in Harmony! Our goal: to create and perfect a cohesive, smooth-functioning team, which by virtue of its harmony of action, unity of purpose and its invincible determination, will be able to out-point the enemy on every count."

minutes, and run 1.5 miles (2.4 km) in 13.3 minutes. Females must do a flexed-arm hang for twelve seconds, complete forty-four crunches in two minutes, and run 1.5 miles (2.4 km) in fifteen minutes. If you fail, you'll be sent to Physical Conditioning Platoon (PCP) and stay there until you pass the test before you can join other recruits at boot camp.

You'll meet your drill sergeants and endure marching in formation as a group, called close-order drills, from day one, even though you won't technically start training for a few days after your arrival. This will get you into the habit of moving together as one entity—a team so wholly united, it becomes an unstoppable, formidable force. A platoon must smoothly, effortlessly, and rapidly respond to a drill instructor's commands.

LEARNING WHAT "HARD WORK" REALLY MEANS

After processing, your training starts in earnest. Throughout the next twelve weeks, you'll go through:

- Close-order drills to build cohesion and confidence. Your platoon will be tested in weeks five and eleven.
- Obstacle courses, individually and in teams, to build upper-body strength and agility, as well as teamwork skills.

- Combat conditioning to strengthen your core and develop correct martial arts technique.
- Conditioning marches in full gear to build endurance. These will increase over time from 3 miles (4.8 km) to 9 miles (14.5 km).
- Classroom instruction on military history, Marine Corps customs and courtesies, first aid, and standards of professionalism while in uniform.

Recruits also learn the eleven leadership principles, fourteen leadership traits, and the Marine Corps' core values: honor, courage, and commitment. These lessons will guide every action and decision you make as a marine.

Other skills are broken down into different weeks. In the early weeks recruits learn the Marine Corps Martial Arts Program (MCMAP). This combination of various martial arts styles teaches you how to defend yourself and disarm your opponent in close combat situations.

Early on you'll train with pugil sticks. These heavily padded poles simulate a rifle and bayonet when used in one-on-one combat. You may have seen them on shows like *American Gladiator* or even had inflatable or toy pugil sticks as a child. The sticks you will use are about 40 inches (102 cm) long and weigh

Pugil stick training is among the first training steps recruits take. The pugil stick acts as rifle and bayonet. The exercises mimic hand-to-hand combat in a safe-but-still-intense environment.

around 9 pounds (4.1 kilograms)—the same as an M16 rifle, the standard Marine Corps weapon. You'll spar with other recruits and learn how to overpower and outmaneuver your opponent.

Sounds easy and even fun, right? Try sparring while also balancing on a slim bridge or in a tight trench with little elbow room. Some graduates say pugil training is the toughest, most intense part of boot camp.

Pugil stick training is broken down into three levels. In the first part, you learn safety tips and rules. In part two, you'll spar on those wooden bridges elevated about 2.5 feet (.8 m) off the ground. In part three, you'll take your training to those tight trenches.

Once you master the pugil stick, you'll move on to actual bayonets. The bayonet is a removable knife attached to the muzzle of your rifle barrel. You'll learn to quickly attach and detach the bayonet. You'll also learn both offensive and defensive fighting techniques.

Remember, marines consider themselves riflemen first and foremost. Bayonet and pugil stick training prepares you for two crucial weeks of boot camp: rifle training.

The M16 is a marine's life force. You'll handle your rifle often. Close-order drills train your platoon to move as one, but they also make you comfortable with your rifle. You'll get so used to it moving in your hands and around your body that it's as if the rifle is another limb. It should respond to your commands in fractions of a second.

Rifle training is broken into two weeklong programs. During Grass Week, you'll learn safety basics and work on marksmanship. You'll practice firing without ammunition in four positions: sitting, kneeling, standing, and lying prone. This week your goal is to fire with precision and ease.

THE SILENT DRILL PLATOON

When the Silent Drill Platoon moves into action, sounds fade to nothingness. Their crisp dress blues form a backdrop for rifle acrobatics. There are no commands for when to turn or how to move their rifles. You only hear the click of shoes on the floor and slap of metal and wood against leather gloves.

This handpicked platoon embodies the spirit of the Marine Corps—the graceful, effortless, rapid drills of many moving as one without a need for voiced commands. They perform across the country in silent precision, using disciplined practice and eye contact as their rifles swirl and twirl through the air. They are based at the United States' oldest active post, Marine Barracks, Washington, D.C., which is also home of the commandant of the Marine Corps and "The Commandant's Own."

Week two is Firing Week. You will use live rounds and fire in all four positions. This week's goal is accuracy. You must be able to consistently hit your target at 200 yards (183 m), 300 yards (274 m), and 500 yards (457 m). You'll start with fifty rounds, one shot at a time, and build up to rapid fire, or ten quickly fired shots in a row.

The last day of Firing Week is Qualification Day. You will be tested and scored on marksmanship. Your goal this day is to get as close to 250 points as possible. Based on your performance, you'll earn your rifle badge: the Rifle Marksman badge, the Rifle Sharpshooter badge, or the best of the best—the Crossed Rifles Expert badge. If you don't do as well as you'd hoped, don't fret. As a marine, you must qualify again each year.

OTHER ESSENTIAL SKILLS

Of course, rifles aren't the only aspects of combat that recruits must master. During boot camp, you'll also experience gas mask training, combat water survival, rappelling, and basic warrior training.

Gas mask training teaches you how to protect yourself and remain calm during a chemical or biological attack. You'll use the M40 field protective mask and sit with fellow recruits in a gas chamber filled with nonlethal CS gas. This is a type of gas often used in riot control. It won't kill you, but it will push you mentally and physically.

Part of your training will be combat water survival. Marines are an amphibious military force. They attack from water and land. You'll need to feel as confident in the ocean or a river as you do on land. You'll train while wearing your gear and supplies. You'll also learn survival swim strokes and other survival techniques, as well as water rescue and first aid. Higher-level recruits may train in full combat gear, including rifle, helmet, flak jacket, and pack.

Marine recruits learn to descend by rappelling, a controlled slide technique. Active-duty marines rappel from buildings, mountainsides, and helicopters to quickly deploy and move into action.

Marines don't only charge in by land and water. Sometimes they need to deploy from helicopters. Rappelling is a controlled slide down a rope. This skill has other uses as well, such as moving around rough terrain or entering buildings during a raid.

To safely rappel, you must learn how to slow or speed up as needed, how to brake, and most important, how to land safely. Marine Corps depots have rappelling towers for training. That first drop might make your stomach clench, but by the end of training you'll be sliding down that rope as easily as you climb stairs.

CONFIDENCE COURSES

You'll face eleven challenges in two Confidence Courses. There are two rounds. You'll go through them on your own and in what's called a four-man fire team. Fire teams are small, flexible combatant teams first used by marines in World War II.

Each challenge, you'll find, is more demanding than the one before it. On your own it's tough; in a fire team, you must work together to succeed.

In Confidence Course I, you'll test your strength and balance with the arm stretcher, parallel bars, and over-and-under obstacles. In Confidence Course II, you'll face higher obstacles, such as a skyscraper, an A-frame, and a little something called the Slide for Life. You might think it sounds like a playground, but success takes strength, courage, and determination.

When they say slide, they mean slide, barehanded, along a rope—a long, thick, difficult-to-grasp rope suspended between two 30-foot (9 m) towers and swaying high above a muddy pond.

Basic Warrior training teaches you how to operate in combat. The infiltration techniques you'll learn include how to prepare personal equipment for battle, getting past barbed wire, hand and arm signals so that you can communicate silently, and how to identify mines or other explosives. You'll also learn the three C's: camouflage, cover, and concealment. Land navigation training will teach you map positioning using landmarks and how to use a lensatic compass and military topographic map.

Nearly twelve weeks of drills, marches, yelling, shooting, gassing, climbing, running, twisting, and strategizing will culminate in the last days of boot camp. Those days are called the Crucible.

THE ULTIMATE TEST

The Crucible is unique to the Marine Corps. It's fifty-four straight hours of mental and physical tests that push you to the brink. During the Crucible, you can prove that you have what it takes. You and your team will face stark conditions, including little food and even less sleep. Together you must infiltrate opponents' territory, conduct resupply and casualty evacuations, fire in combat scenarios, and more. You'll be issued challenges that you must solve quickly as a team and with minimal tools. And you'll march. And march. And march. Throughout almost-two-and-a-half days, you'll need to make choices and act upon your Marine Corps core values training.

If you succeed, at the end of those fifty-four hours, your platoon will march together in the Emblem Ceremony. At that time, your drill instructor will present you with the eagle, globe, and anchor. Finally, you will have earned the right to call yourself a U.S. Marine.

ADVANCED INDIVIDUAL TRAINING (AIT)

About eleven days after you receive the emblem, you'll start advanced training for your Military Occupational Specialty, or MOS. Your MOS depends upon the results of the ASVAB you took during enlistment, plus such factors as available openings and the Marine Corps' needs.

AIT occurs at different bases across the country. For example, infantrymen attend the Infantry Training Battalion Course at the School of Infantry East at Camp Geiger in Jacksonville, North Carolina, or the School of Infantry West at Camp Pendleton in San Diego, California. AIT, can take a few weeks and up to several months. We'll discuss more in the following chapters.

Marksmanship is one of the most crucial skills a marine can have. Recruits train two out of the twelve weeks on shooting skills. Once certified, a marine must retest each year to stay certified.

After completing AIT, you'll receive your base assignment. There are eleven permanent Marine Corps bases, which will be your home for the next several years, regardless of where you might be deployed:

- Camp Butler, Okinawa, Japan
- MCACGG Twentynine Palms, Twentynine Palms, California
- MCB Camp Pendleton, Oceanside, California

- MCB Hawaii, Honolulu, Hawaii
- MCAS Miramar, San Diego, California
- MCAS Yuma, Yuma, Arizona
- Marine Barracks, Washington, D.C.
- MCB Quantico, Quantico, Virginia
- MCAS New River and MCB Camp Lejeune, Jacksonville, North Carolina
- MCAS Cherry Point, Cherry Point, North Carolina
- MCAS Beaufort, Beaufort, South Carolina

CHAPTER 3

Latitude ➤ 44° 49' 6

Longitude ➤ 20° 28'

COMBAT SPECIALTIES

Marines chosen for combat specialties are the best of the warriors. They are considered experts at weapons, martial arts, battlefield tactics, and survival. Enlisted personnel train in three areas: field artillery, infantry, and tank and amphibian armor. Officers can train to be pilots as well. As of February 2011, women marines can train in combat specialties but cannot serve in units whose main mission is to engage and fight in direct combat.

FIELD ARTILLERY

Have you ever watched a war movie where a team of soldiers unloads crate after crate of equipment from a truck, then reassembles all the pieces into a weapon on the field? Those soldiers are field artillery marines. They form the infantry's foundation.

Marines load a round into the M777 Light Towed Howitzer. Field exercises train them to rapidly load and accurately fire. Exercise targets include firing in a grenade range and a combat marksmanship range.

They are trained to operate and maintain all artillery equipment, including weapons such as cannons. But they also need the knowledge to evaluate data to ensure a battle plan can succeed.

After recruit training, enlisted and officer field artillery marines travel to the army's Fort Sill in Oklahoma to receive MOS training in one of three areas: firing battery, field artillery operations, and field artillery observation/liaison.

Firing battery jobs include loading, transporting, protecting, and firing field artillery cannon weapons systems. Marines in this field must know how to camouflage all the weapons. They inspect and prepare ammunition, as well as prepare the cannon for firing. They must keep all artillery pieces clean, and they must perform regular tests in order to ensure that everything works properly.

Field artillery operations also maintain, transport, and fire equipment, but these soldiers evaluate all kinds of information, including weather, to analyze weapon system performance. They convey orders to the firing battery.

Marines trained in field artillery observation and liaison will analyze combat plans and communicate all planning and operating information to other marines. They coordinate the fires of field artillery and naval guns with infantry and armor combat maneuvers. They observe and report targets and other battlefield information.

Entry-level jobs include field artillery batteryman or cannoneer, radar operator, fire control man, and meteorological man. Other jobs include high-mobility artillery rocket system operator and field artillery fire control man. A fire support man uses laser designators, range finders, and radar beacons.

MEDAL OF HONOR RECIPIENT SERGEANT MAJOR DANIEL "DAN" JOSEPH DALY

The marines fighting at Belleau Wood on June 6, 1918, were outnumbered and trapped. The Germans were bearing down hard. When the order came to attack, then Gunnery Sergeant Daniel Daly ignited his men by leaping up and crying out, "Do you want to live forever?"

The marine losses that day were huge, but the bravery of Daly and thousands of others helped turn the tide in that fateful World War I battle.

Daly had already earned two Medals of Honor before Belleau Wood. He is one of just seven marines awarded two medals, and only one of two to have earned them for two separate actions.

He'd been pinned down and outnumbered before. As a private fighting in the Boxer Rebellion in China in 1900, Daly single-handedly fought off Chinese snipers who stormed his position with just his rifle and bayonet until others arrived. That earned him his first Medal of Honor.

Fifteen years later he earned his second fighting Haitian rebels alongside Major General Smedley Butler, the only other two-time Medal recipient honored for two different actions. Butler called Daly "the fightingest marine I've ever known."

Ever low-key about his accomplishments, Sergeant Major Daly is said to have called the fourteen medals he earned "a lot of foolishness." He turned down commissions more than once, supposedly noting he'd rather be an outstanding sergeant than just another officer. Major General John Lejeune, former commandant of the Marine Corps, called Daly "the outstanding marine of all time."

Sergeant Major Dan Daley was born in Glen Cove, New York, on November 11, 1873. He enlisted in the Marine Corps on January 10, 1899, and retired on February 6, 1929. He passed away on April 28, 1937. Six years after his death, the USS *Dan Daly* (DD519), a destroyer, was commissioned on March 10, 1943. She sailed around the world until 1960.

INFANTRY

Infantry is the main part of the Marine Corps' ground forces. These are the marines you likely picture in your mind, ever vigilant with M16s in hand, who patrol dangerous perimeters, infiltrate enemy grounds, and engage in direct combat. Their reputation precedes them: the U.S. Marine Corps Infantry is considered to be the best in close combat. It's filled with marines of astounding courage under fire. They train to locate and destroy the enemy and defend against attacks. Within each infantry unit are riflemen who act as scouts and specialize in close combat. Other jobs include machine gunner, mortarman, infantry rifleman, and antitank missile operator.

After recruit training, infantrymen attend the Infantry Training Battalion Course for five weeks. Those who graduate from Parris Island attend the School of Infantry East at Camp Geiger. Those who graduate from San Diego attend the School of Infantry West at Camp Pendleton.

There are four jobs within infantry. Riflemen are trained in close combat with the M16A4 rifle. They also use M203 grenade launchers and the squad automatic weapon. Machine gunners use medium and heavy machine guns. Mortarmen use light or medium mortars to support gunners and riflemen. Assaultmen fire rockets, perform demolitions, and conduct breach and infiltration techniques.

ARMOR

Armor marines are the heavy machinery guys. As crewmen, they man 70-ton (63 metric-ton) M1A1 Abrams tanks and amphibious assault vehicles (AAVs). They form a power shield for ground forces.

AAV platoons perform all ship-to-shore operations. Each one can transport twenty-four marines or 10,000 pounds (4,536 kg) of cargo through the choppiest of waters and most hostile of lands. All AAV crewmen complete the Assault Amphibian Crewman Course at Camp Pendleton. There can be up to seventeen AAVs supporting ground operations. Within the seventeen are the command AAV crew that

The Marine Corps M1 Abrams Main Battle Tank is called the backbone of the U.S. heavy armored force. Marine armored forces train to drive, fire, and maintain this massive tank.

coordinates radios and communications and a recovery AAV crew that handles repairs or maintenance.

Tank crewmen travel to Fort Knox in Kentucky to undergo the M1A1 Crewman Course. There they learn how to operate, maintain, fire, and gracefully maneuver the lumbering tanks. Within the platoon are three different tasks. The tank gunner prepares the tanks, marines, and equipment for movement and combat. He also locates targets and uses the weapons

A MARINE IS FIRST AND FOREMOST A RIFLEMAN

The attacks on Pearl Harbor in December 1942 inspired Major General William Rupertus to write "My Rifle: The Creed of a U.S. Marine." This embodies the special relationship marines have with their rifles.

This is my rifle. There are many like it, but this one is mine. My rifle is my best friend. It is my life. I must master it as I must master my life.

My rifle, without me, is useless. Without my rifle, I am useless. I must fire my rifle true. I must shoot straighter than my enemy who is trying to kill me. I must shoot him before he shoots me. I will . . .

My rifle and myself know that what counts in this war is not the rounds we fire, the noise of our burst, nor the smoke we make. We know that it is the hits that count. We will hit . . .

My rifle is human, even as I, because it is my life. Thus, I will learn it as a brother. I will learn its weaknesses, its strength, its parts, its accessories, its sights and its barrel. I will ever guard it against the ravages of weather and damage as I will ever guard my legs, my arms, my eyes and my heart against damage. I will keep my rifle clean and ready. We will become part of each other. We will . . .

Before God, I swear this creed. My rifle and myself are the defenders of my country. We are the masters of our enemy. We are the saviors of my life. So be it, until victory is America's and there is no enemy, but peace!

systems. The tank driver does just that: drives the tank during movement and positions the tank for optimal targeting. He also performs maintenance and operational duties as needed. The tank commander supervises all maintenance and operations. As the leader, he is responsible for the vehicle and crew. Each platoon includes four M1A1 Abrams battle tanks and one M88A1 tank recovery vehicle.

SAPPERS

Sappers are specially trained to penetrate enemy defenses and clear a path into a combat area using explosives, trenches, or other field fortifications. Sapper training is a six-week-long engineering course at Camp Pendleton that teaches marines additional combat techniques. Plus, they get extra training in high explosives and field maneuverings. It's broken down into five phases: land navigation and communication, patrolling techniques, reconnaissance, land mines and mine warfare, and explosives and demolition.

CHAPTER 4

VEHICLE/MACHINERY AND MECHANICS

The vehicle/machinery and mechanics MOS is perfect for grease monkeys. However, this isn't like working on an old Toyota. Specializing in this occupational field means you'll learn to repair and modify all air and ground support vehicles used by the Marine Corps. An elite group services Marine One and Marine Two—the helicopters used by the president and vice president of the United States. There isn't just one designated helicopter. An entire marine fleet serves the president. The call signs refer to the specific marine aircraft that is at that time transporting the president or vice president. A maintenance crew of eight hundred is based in Quantico, Virginia.

The two main areas are aircraft maintenance and motor transport maintenance, but each requires multiple skills and offers all kinds of learning opportunities.

Aviation ordnance technicians prepare the AH-1W Super Cobra helicopter for service. These marines, based at Udairi Airfield, Kuwait, bore-sight the M-220 Tube-launched Optically tracked Wire-guided missile system.

AIRCRAFT MAINTENANCE

Marines who specialize in aircraft maintenance learn skills to ensure that all aircraft, from helicopters to fighter jets, work properly. The areas in which you can specialize vary. You might be selected to train in pre-flight servicing, hydraulics, wing maintenance, frame maintenance, or myriad other options. Some occupational fields provide apprenticeship opportunities that let you specialize even further. As you move up in rank, you might have opportunities to serve at the wing and force commander levels.

Officers can serve as air traffic control managers and aircraft maintenance managers. Enlisted aircrews prepare the aircraft and oversee all functions during missions and in-flight refueling. They perform navigational duties, operate and maintain communications systems, and load equipment. Here's a small glimpse at the diverse specialties available:

- Aviation maintenance controller/production controller
- Aircraft maintenance chief
- Aircraft power plants test cell operator
- Aircraft nondestructive inspection technician
- Aircraft welder
- Flight equipment technician
- Aircraft intermediate level hydraulic/pneumatic mechanic
- Cryogenics equipment operator
- Aircraft intermediate level structures mechanic
- Helicopter mechanic
- Tiltrotor mechanic
- Helicopter power plants mechanic
- Helicopter airframe mechanic

MARINE NICKNAMES: BADGES OF HONOR

Marines go by several nicknames. Perhaps the best known is "jarhead," which comes from a marine's distinct high-and-tight haircut combined with the high collar of the dress uniform. Legend says World War II sailors made fun of how marines' heads rose from their stiff collars by calling them "jarheads." The marines adopted the slur as a badge of honor.

The high collar had been around since the late 1700s, when the earliest marines wore a stiff leather collar. Some say it was designed to keep a marine's head erect and proud, while others say the leather protected the neck from the slashes of enemy swords. The leather collar stopped being part of the uniform in 1872, but marines still call themselves "leathernecks."

Enemy respect and fear led to other nicknames. Legend says Germans battling the marines at Belleau Wood in World War I reported that they had fought a shock troop of *teufelhunden*, or "devil dogs." The khaki leggings worn by marines during the Korean War were so distinct that the Communist forces supposedly were ordered to avoid the fierce "yellowlegs."

"Grunt" isn't unique to marines. All military infantrymen are called "grunts" because they grunt when lifting their gear onto their backs—loads upward to 125 pounds (57 kg)—before heading into battle. Less-friendly folk say it's because infantrymen grunt to communicate. But marines consider the name a badge of honor. Infantrymen represent the courage and stamina needed in a warrior marine.

- Presidential support specialist
- Helicopter crew chief
- Presidential helicopter crew chief
- Enlisted aircrew/aerial observer/gunner
- Fixed-wing aircraft mechanic
- Fixed-wing aircraft flight engineer

After recruit training, you will move on to your MOS training at Cherry Point, North Carolina; Milton, Florida; Fort Huachuca, Arizona; or Camp Pendleton, California. You might complete an equivalent OMA Contractors Maintenance, Aircrew, or Air Vehicle Operators Course. The skills you learn are in demand in the civilian world, too. After you leave the Marine Corps, you can get a job as an aircraft mechanic, electrician, hydraulics specialist, aviation machinist, sheet metal worker, and more.

MOTOR MAINTENANCE

Motor maintenance training prepares marines to repair and maintain all tactical motor vehicles and amphibian trucks used by the force. Several training courses available are offered at Camp Lejeune, including:

- AOMC – Automotive Organizational Maintenance Course

Even a Humvee can't travel through rugged terrain and rushing waters without a little help. Marines trained in vehicle/machinery and mechanics maintain the equipment for all motor and aircraft transports.

- AIMC – Automotive Intermediate Maintenance Course
- MILMO – Military Motorcycle Course
- LVSMC – Logistics Vehicle System Maintenance Course
- FESCRC – Fuel and Electrical Systems Component Repair Course

A motor transport platoon transports marines and supplies all units in the Marine Air Ground Task Force (MAGTF). They use 7-ton (6.4-metric-ton) trucks and high-mobility multipurpose wheeled vehicles, or HMMWVs—known in the civilian world as Humvees. They also provide fuel and water tankers and operate wreckers as needed to recover vehicles or handle lifting and towing. Officers serve as traffic managers and automotive maintenance managers. Enlisted jobs include:

- Automotive organizational mechanic
- Automotive intermediate mechanic
- Logistics vehicle system mechanic
- Fuel and electrical systems mechanic
- Crash/fire/rescue vehicle mechanic
- Motor transport maintenance chief
- Motor vehicle operator
- Logistics vehicle system operator

TANKS IN AFGHANISTAN

The first tanks to serve in the "War on Terror" arrived at Camp Leatherneck, Afghanistan, in January 2011. The M1A1 tanks were specially upgraded since they were last used in Operation Desert Storm in the early 1990s. The new upgrade includes a 120mm M256 cannon and a nuclear/biological/chemical overpressure system that will protect the passengers from attack. An improved fire control system and other upgrades means the M1A1 can shoot more accurately on the move.

The new smoothbore cannon uses armor-defeating ammunition to accurately hit targets up to 13,123 feet (4,000 m) away. The four-man tank crew includes a commander, gunner, loader, and driver. The commander's station has six periscopes that give a 360-degree view. The gunner uses a night-vision thermal imaging system that uses radiant heat to create an image. The driver sits in a semireclined position and has three observation periscopes that together provide a 120-degree view. One is equipped with night vision, which means the driver can still have a clear view, even at night or in the poor visibility conditions of a smoky or dusty battlefield. The turret has two six-barreled M250 smoke grenade launchers that act as a clocking device to mask the heat of the tank.

Tank maintenance crews spend about the same amount of time servicing and maintaining the tank as the armor crew spends in action. Four hours of patrol means four hours of maintenance to ensure the tank is ready for action.

- Semitrailer refueler operator
- Vehicle recovery operator
- Motor transport operations chief
- Licensing examiner

Military machines come equipped with the latest technological advances. When you work on a HMMWV in the Marine Corps, you'll learn techniques and skills that you can use later in your civilian life as an automotive mechanic, automotive engineer, electrical systems specialist, and more.

CHAPTER 5

ELECTRONIC/ ELECTRICAL SYSTEMS

Many of the most technically complex and exciting jobs are found in the electronic and electrical system field. Depending upon the results of your tests, you might be assigned to train in avionics, data communications maintenance, electronics maintenance, or training and audiovisual support. These jobs require intensive, specialized, and ongoing training. Many also require you to have security clearance from the U.S. Department of Defense. There are three different levels of security clearance:

- Confidential: Information or material that could potentially damage national security if it's revealed
- Secret: Information or material that if revealed could seriously damage national security

- Top secret: Information or material that if revealed could cause exceptionally grave damage to national security

Higher-level specialties require confidential and secret security clearance and in some cases require top-secret clearance. You must achieve the rank of sergeant or higher before you can train for jobs that require security clearance.

AVIONICS

Marines who train in avionics learn to install, maintain, and repair all aviation weapons and electrical systems. They perform preflight checks and inspections and handle all repairs after each mission, plus support communications, including radar and navigational systems. The avionics training course takes six months and is held in Pensacola, Florida. These jobs require confidential security clearance at minimum, and for many jobs secret security clearance is needed.

You can specialize in specific areas within avionics as well. Avionics Test Set (ATS) technicians inspect, test, maintain,

This avionics technician tests connections on the CH-53E Super Stallion. This heavy lift helicopter transports personnel and equipment, and it supports special operations and combat rescue missions.

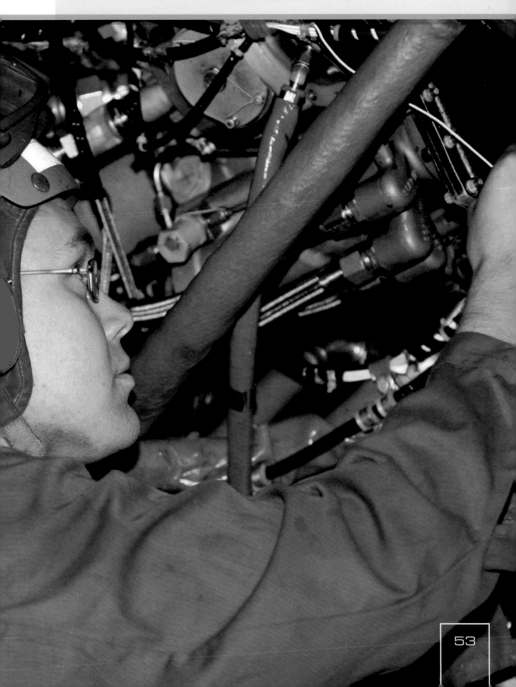

and repair aircraft weapons systems. Aircraft communications/navigation/electrical systems technicians train to manage electrical systems, components, and ancillary equipment. For example, some technicians work only on the V-22 Osprey. The Osprey aircraft is a multimission aircraft designed specifically for military use. It takes off and lands like a helicopter, which makes it flexible in combat situations, but it can fly long-range like a plane. It holds about twenty-four troops or up to 20,000 pounds (9,072 kg) of cargo. It's great for search and rescue, and it can easily be transported aboard aircraft carriers because its rotors can fold and the wings rotate.

Aircraft electronic countermeasures systems technicians operate defensive systems, such as jammers and missiles. One such aircraft is the EA-6B, a twin-engine airplane designed for electronic warfare. It can jam enemy radio systems and be used to gather intelligence. It also can carry and fire antiradiation missiles. Other jobs:

- Unmanned aerial system avionics technician
- Aircraft communications/navigation systems technician
- Aircraft communications/navigation/radar systems technician
- Aircraft communications/navigation/electrical systems technician

THE MARINES' HYMN

You probably grew up hearing the inspiring "Marines' Hymn," which starts out declaring "From the halls of Montezuma to the shores of Tripoli." You may not have known those referred to actual battles fought by U.S. Marines and are inscribed in the official flag of the Marine Corps.

"To the shores of Tripoli" was first added to the marine colors after a war with the Barbary Pirates in 1805. "From the halls of Montezuma" was added after marines helped capture Mexico City and the Castle of Chapultepec (known as the Halls of Montezuma) in 1847.

You also likely didn't know the "Marines' Hymn" is the oldest of our country's military service songs. Legend says the music is from a comic opera composed by Jacques Offenbach in 1859. No one is sure who wrote the actual words. Some say an unknown marine wrote a poem in 1847. An early version of the hymn was declared the official "Marines' Hymn" in 1929. In 1942, Commandant Thomas Holcomb approved a change in the first verse from "on land as on the sea" to "in the air, on land, and sea." The hymn remains:

"From the Halls of Montezuma to the shores of Tripoli;
We fight our country's battles in the air, on land,
*   and sea;*
First to fight for right and freedom and to keep our
*   honor clean;*
We are proud to claim the title of United States
*   Marine.*

(CONTINUED ON PAGE 56)

THE MARINES' HYMN (CONTINUED)

Our flag's unfurled to every breeze from dawn to
    setting sun;
We have fought in ev'ry clime and place where we
    could take a gun;
In the snow of far-off Northern lands and in sunny
    tropic scenes;
You will find us always on the job. The United States
    Marines

Here's health to you and to our Corps which we are
    proud to serve;
In many a strife we've fought for life and never lost
    our nerve;
If the Army and the Navy ever look on Heaven's
    scenes;
They will find the streets are guarded by United
    States Marines."

- Aircraft communications/navigation/electrical/ weapons systems technician
- Aircraft electrical systems technician
- Aircraft electronic countermeasures systems technician
- Avionics maintenance chief
- Advanced aircraft communications/navigation systems technician
- Aircraft cryptographic systems technician
- Aviation electronic microminiature/instrument and cable repair technician

- Aircraft electrical/instrument/flight control systems technician, fixed wing
- Aircraft electrical/instrument/flight control systems technician, helicopter
- Advanced aircraft electrical/instrument/ flight control systems technician
- Hybrid Test Set (HTS) technician
- Avionics Test Set (ATS) technician
- Consolidated Automatic Support System (CASS) technician
- CASS HP configuration operator/ maintainer/technician
- Aircraft inertial navigation system technician
- CASS EO configuration operator/ maintainer/technician
- CASS test station IMA advanced mainte- nance technician
- Aircraft electronic countermeasures systems technician, fixed-wing
- Aircraft electronic countermeasures systems technician, helicopter
- CASS EW configuration operator/ maintainer/technician
- Aviation precision measurement equipment/ calibration and repair technician
- Aviation meteorological equipment technician

A radio operator prepares ground sensors used to monitor movement, sounds, and vibrations in the field. Modern warfare relies on data communications. Ground sensor platoons keep vital communications equipment working.

DATA COMMUNICATIONS MAINTENANCE

Marines who train in data communications maintenance learn how to install and repair electronic equipment and systems. They can diagnose problems and adjust, calibrate, or modify the equipment to suit a particular goal. The different equipment includes ground radar, electronics used to detect nuclear or biological weaponry, cryptographic devices, unmanned aerial vehicles, and more. After recruit training, marines in this field will attend communications systems training at Twentynine Palms, California. Communications marines serve throughout the Marine Air Ground Task Force.

Marines chosen for this specialty have exceptional manual dexterity and understand complex mathematical and logic principles. Like many careers in the military, you aren't eligible if you are color-blind. Entry-level enlisted jobs include ground

SEMPER FI

Semper Fidelis is Latin for "Always Faithful." It is the Marine Corps motto, declared on the anchor, eagle, and globe emblem. In two words it sums up twelve weeks of boot camp training, the Crucible, the weeks or months of advanced training, the years of service, the core values, the gung-ho nature of this particular military force, and the experiences shared with fellow marines.

The Marine Corps adopted Semper Fidelis as its official motto in 1883. This wasn't the first motto. Fortitudine—"With Courage"—was used around the War of 1812. For a time, U.S. Marines adopted the British Royal Marines motto Per mare, per terram—"By sea, by land." There was also the famous motto "To the shores of Tripoli," which is inscribed on the Marine Corps flag, as well as sung in its hymn.

But Semper Fidelis embodied all the rich meaning of these other words and so much more. Becoming a marine changes who you are, how you look at the world, and the standards to which you will forever hold yourself long after your time as an active marine ends.

You'll hear it often: there is no such thing as an ex-marine. Once you earn the right to call yourself a marine, you will forever be a marine. No matter how long ago they served, marines cry out the words "semper fi!" with fervor. Semper Fi to the mission. Semper Fi to the United States of America. Semper Fi to the Corps and all marines past, present, and future.

communications repairer, personal computer repairer, and artillery electronics technician. Other jobs are the field radio operator, who sets up and operates all radio equipment used in a field mission, and the data network specialist, who installs, configures, and maintains network services, including both hardware and software.

Higher-level specialties include artillery electronics technicians, who maintain the AN/TPQ-36 counter mortar radar system, the AN/TMQ-41 meteorological measuring system (MMS), the M-94 Chronograph (MVS), and the ancillary ground radar systems. Satellite communications (SATCOM) technicians are qualified to test and repair satellite communications equipment. You will need secret clearance to train in these specialties.

Tactical electronic reconnaissance process/evaluation systems (TERPES) technicians are responsible for all technical duties required for the maintenance of the systems. TERPES technicians need top-secret security clearance.

Ground communications organizational repairers diagnose problems with electronic equipment and repair or adjust it as needed for a mission. Some of the specialties in this area are electronic switching equipment technician, multichannel communications equipment repairer, ground communications organizational repairer, and telephone system/personal computer repairer, among other jobs.

Other jobs in data communications maintenance include:

- Technical controller marine
- Electronic switching equipment technician
- Technical control chief
- AN/TRC-170 technician
- Telephone systems/personal computer intermediate repairer
- Tactical Remote Sensor System (TRSS) maintainer
- Electronics maintenance technician
- Test measurement and diagnostic equipment technician
- Metrology technician
- 2M/ATE technician

ELECTRONICS MAINTENANCE

Marines chosen to train in electronics maintenance operate and repair equipment within the Marine Air Command and Control Systems, Marine Aircraft Wing. They work on sophisticated equipment systems for air defense and surveillance radar systems, aviation radio communications, air traffic control systems, tactical data systems, and short-range air defense weapon systems. Like data communications maintenance, many of these jobs are open to higher-ranking marines and require differing levels of security clearance. Jobs include:

Staff Sergeant Joshua Hooten works as an air traffic controller at the ATC tower at the Marine Corps Air Station in Yuma, Arizona.

- Avenger system maintainer
- Aviation communications systems technician
- Aviation radar repairer
- Aviation radar technician
- Air traffic control navigational aids technician
- Air traffic control radar technician
- Air traffic control communications technician
- Air traffic control systems maintenance
- Tactical data systems administrator
- Tactical air operations module/air defense technician
- Electronics maintenance chief

Military photographers photograph the damage on a main street after a battle in Fallujah, Iraq. Military photographers document history and help the military in tactical planning for future maneuvers.

TRAINING AND AUDIOVISUAL SUPPORT

Are you artistic? Do you have skills with a still or video camera? Would you like to capture what military life is really like? You might be right for an audiovisual support specialty. Any visual information, such as graphic arts, training devices, photographic operations, and videography, falls under the training and audiovisual support occupational specialty. A marine with particular artistic and mechanical skills may serve as a combat illustrator, photographer, videographer, or lithographer. Depending on the area, you might train at the Defense Information School in Fort Meade, Maryland, or the Defense Mapping School at Fort Belvoir, Virginia.

CHAPTER 6

PERSONNEL AND BASE SUPPORT

O nce you join the Marine Corps, you'll move to a home base. A Marine Corps base is huge enough to be its own town, complete with a separate ZIP code. It functions much like a college campus. There are training classrooms and shooting ranges, barracks (sort of like dorms), and gymnasiums. There are baseball diamonds and clothing shops.

Most unmarried soldiers live on base in barracks. Those with families live in larger house units, although a small number of unmarried soldiers might also get assigned to a house. Where you are assigned to stay is based on your pay grade and family size. If you cannot live in base housing, you'll receive what's called BAH—basic allowance for housing—to help offset the cost of renting off base. Whether you live dorm-style in the barracks or in an apartment or house, you'll need the services found on base.

- Airfield services to keep aircraft log books and flight operations records
- Accounting, auditing, and finance jobs to prepare pay records, process vouchers, and manage other fiscal duties
- Food services in both the commissary and cafeterias
- Legal services, such as paralegals, court reporters, and law clerks, to prepare and review legal documents
- Marine Corps Exchange jobs, including salesclerks, bookkeepers, stockmen, buyers, and so on
- Military police and corrections officers, including guards for military and war prisoners
- Personnel and administration duties, such as administrative assistants, personnel classification clerks, postal clerks, and librarians
- Printing and reproduction jobs, such as letterpress or lithographic offset machine operators
- Public affairs and media liaison jobs to create content for community relations projects, news stories, and to cover duties in the Armed Forces Radio and Television Service (AFRTS)

WOMEN IN THE MARINES: A HISTORY

American women have participated in the military officially and unofficially since the Revolutionary War. The first woman to enlist in the U.S. Marine Corps Reserve was Opha Mae Johnson, who joined in 1918. She and more than three hundred other women served in World War I, though they weren't allowed in war zones. While some things haven't changed in the last one hundred years—women still can't serve in direct combat—the Marine Corps has seen other changes.

The Marine Corps Women's Reserve was established on July 30, 1942. The roles of these approximately twenty thousand women changed in 1943 to cover typically male shore duties so that more men could ship overseas. Women worked in more than two hundred jobs, including radio operator, parachute rigger, aerial gunner inspector, cryptographer, control tower operator, and drivers.

The first director of the Marine Corps Women's Reserve was Ruth Cheney Streeter. She was commissioned into service in January 1943 and retired as a colonel three years later. The first female marine to receive a commission was Captain Anne Lentz in 1943. She was a clothing expert who helped design Marine Corps uniforms.

Captain Charlotte Day Gower was the second woman commissioned as an officer. The former dean of women at Lingnan University in Hong Kong had been captured by Japanese forces when they invaded the city in 1938. She was a prisoner in an internment camp for five months. After she returned to the United States in 1942, she joined the Marine Corps Women's Reserve and later served as director of training.

After World War II ended, General Alexander Vandegrift, the commandant of the Marine Corps, retained one thousand women to remain on active duty. In the decades since, standards changed so that women could enlist and serve as equals with male marines.

These job assignments might seem bland compared to avionics or artillery divisions, but the training you get on base prepares you for life outside of the Marine Corps. In four years, you'll have plenty to put on your civilian résumé.

Base support jobs are secondary to your main role as a marine—a combat rifleman, ready to deploy at a moment's notice to use your warrior training for the good of your country. Marines train to deploy within six hours of receiving orders. They usually have lots more time before needing to leave base, but in urgent cases marines can be packed up and headed to transports in less time than it takes for you to start and finish a school day.

Each base leader, usually a general or a colonel, creates a supportive and challenging environment to keep marines in peak condition. This is General James F. Amos, 35th commandant of the Marine Corps.

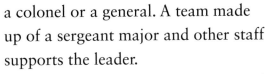

BASE LEADERSHIP

Every base has a team, called the command element, to lead operations and planning. The main leader is

a colonel or a general. A team made up of a sergeant major and other staff supports the leader.

Officer careers within the command element include personnel and administration, intelligence, training and operations, logistics, and communications. Other support personnel work in special operations and public affairs as chaplains, or in legal services and other roles to serve the commander.

Common leadership roles include the adjutant, who manages the record keeping and base procedures and administration. The public affairs office acts as the official spokesperson and leads community relations efforts. Intelligence divisions of human intelligence, signals intelligence, and counterintelligence collect critical information related to national security. Legal services provide operation and management support to the base's legal team.

WOMEN IN THE MARINES: BREAKING BARRIERS

In many circumstances, women have had to train with more intensity and work twice as hard to be considered equal among men. These female marines were the first among their peers:

- Staff Sergeant Barbara Barnwell became the first female marine to receive the Navy and Marine Corps Medal for heroism in 1953 after saving a fellow marine from drowning.
- In 1960, Geraldine Moran was the first female marine promoted to the highest enlisted rank of E9 when she became Master Gunnery Sergeant.
- A year later, Bertha Billeb was awarded the rank Sergeant Major.
- Colonel Margaret Brewer became a brigadier general in 1978.
- In 1992, General Carol Mutter assumed command of 3rd Force Service Support Group in Okinawa, the first woman to do so at flag level.
- In 1993, 2nd Lieutenant Sarah Deal was the first female marine chosen to train as a pilot. She received her wings in 1995.
- Two years later, female marines were allowed to enter combat training.
- In 2003, Captain Vernice Armour became the first African-American woman to serve as a Marine Corps pilot. She is also the first black female combat pilot with missions in Iraq.

LIFE ON BASE: DEPLOYMENT AND FAMILY STRAIN

The reality of military life is that you will likely be deployed overseas at least once during your years of service. Many marines are deployed multiple times or for tours of duty that take them away from their families and loved ones for months, even years, at a time. There are services on base to help you and your family endure the strain of deployment.

The Family Readiness Program helps the entire family prepare for a mission. They are led by military personnel, trained counselors, and family members. As noted in the Camp Pendleton Family Readiness Program, "Marines have three families: the family they are born into, the family they are sworn into, and the family they are married into. Therefore, family support shall be accessible and provided to marines (regardless of marital status), spouses, children, wards and the designated parents/extended family members of marines."

Skype, handwritten letters, and e-mail don't always cut it during military deployment. Bases provide counseling services, communication, and support for families and marines. Even with preparation and a foundation of support, families left behind suffer the strain of separation. Many children struggle in school when a parent is deployed overseas. Spouses and children report

Deployment overseas creates strain and fears. Marines returning from deployment must readjust to base life. Counseling services help marines and their families during difficult times.

suffering insomnia or anxiety. Sometimes financial issues become overwhelming. Family support programs can offer tutoring, financial counseling, and moral support. Still, the stress doesn't always go away as soon as the marines return home.

You train for active combat to serve as a warrior, defeat our country's enemies, and protect your family and way of life. You believe in your duty with all your heart. At the same time, you can't help but be changed by what you experience, especially in direct combat events. The reality of war is that horrific things may happen right before your eyes. Sometimes they happen to those who have become family to you. They might happen to you, such as a debilitating injury or the mental anguish of seeing others damaged or killed. And sometimes you come back knowing your actions caused horrific things.

Even though they believe in their cause and trust that their missions will create a better, more peaceful world, many soldiers return from their tours of duty suffering from post-traumatic stress disorder (PTSD). Support from family isn't always enough. That's why strong support from the home base is so crucial to help soldiers and families readjust successfully.

You might find that you'd like to support and counsel other marines to manage the stress of military life. Becoming active in the base support programs can lead to additional training and possibly a career as a social worker, nurse, family counselor, financial planner, or psychiatrist.

CHAPTER 7

LOGISTICS AND SUPPLY

Latitude > 44° 49' 6"
Latitude > 20° 28' 5"

Marines need supplies to do their jobs. They need water, ammunition, equipment, food, uniforms, armor, gasoline, and other energy sources. They need to set up camp, and they need vehicles to transport people and equipment. This takes a lot of coordination, hard work, and skill to keep things running smoothly. Marines chosen to work in logistics and supply jobs have some of the most important jobs in the Corps.

LOGISTICS

Marines chosen for logistics jobs handle all equipment acquisitions, storage, and distribution. They move people and construct and maintain facilities around the world. If you're chosen for a job in logistics, you'll attend the Logistics Operations School and the Marine Corps Combat Service Support School at Camp Lejeune.

Marines in a Combat Logistics Regiment load food onto a cargo platform at Marine Corps Air Station Futenma. The marines shipped these supplies to victims of the earthquake and tsunami that struck Japan in 2011.

Logistics marines serve in a Landing Support Platoon. They track and receive all shipments of food, water, fuel, ammunition, equipment, and so on with sophisticated software programs. Some specialties include:

Embarkation specialists: These marines help prepare for strategic transportation operations carried aboard aircraft or ships.

Airborne and air delivery specialists: These marines maintain life safety equipment for all airborne and airdrop operations. For example, parachute riggers work under this specialty.

Landing support specialists: The marines need effective soldiers to maintain and control transportation systems on shores, landing zones, ports, and shipping terminals.

Many logistics jobs require security clearance. Enlisted jobs include administrative clerks, traffic management specialists, and more. Some job titles are:

- Maintenance management specialist
- Logistics/embarkation specialist
- Airborne and air delivery specialist
- Personnel retrieval and processing specialist
- Personnel retrieval and processing technician
- Landing support specialist
- Logistics mobility chief

IN PURSUIT OF KNOWLEDGE

The Marine Corps provides intensive and ongoing training, but sometimes marines want to continue civilian education in their off-duty time. The Marine Corps Tuition Assistance Program is a financial aid program. You could receive up to $4,500 a year to help offset tuition expenses at a civilian school. To be eligible, you must take classes that will lead to a higher academic level than you've already achieved. In other words, if you have an associate's degree you must be working toward a bachelor's degree, and so on.

The Servicemembers Opportunity Colleges are a group of colleges and universities that help military personnel pursue advanced degrees. They have agreed to reduce residency requirements and accept nontraditional tests, such as the College Level Examination Program. This makes it easier to transfer college credits among similarly accredited schools and in many cases grants college credit for formal military training.

SUPPLY ADMINISTRATION

While logistic specialties get things moving, supply administration specialties ensure the forces are supplied with the right goods in the right amounts and that they are properly packaged for shipment. If you're chosen for supply administration training, you'll study the Enlisted Supply Basic Course at Camp Lejeune.

Supply platoons are the central storage and distribution points for most supply line items. These include equipment parts, fuel, rations, and uniforms and other clothing. Some specialties are:

- Supply administration and operations clerks: Like the title says, these marines perform administration duties, including paperwork management and shipment scheduling.
- Warehouse clerks: These marines inspect all supplies as they receive them. They also store the goods and prepare items for shipment as needed for ground support.
- Packaging specialists: These marines prepare and package sensitive materials, such as surveillance equipment, for shipment.

AMMUNITION AND EXPLOSIVES ORDNANCE DISPOSAL

Some of the more intense, skilled jobs in the Marine Corps fall under the ammunition and explosives ordnance disposal specialties. These marines are trained to disarm explosives, such as land mines or bombs. They handle hazardous materials. They also are

An ordnance disposal team in Afghanistan gently places unexploded ordnance in lines to be destroyed safely. The marines work closely with Afghan National Police and Border Police.

trained to inspect, repair, and maintain the many weapons systems in the Marine Corps. They are the military bomb squads.

If you're chosen to serve in an explosives ordnance disposal specialty, you'll complete a technical ordnance course. Some examples are the Enlisted Ammunition Specialist Course in Redstone, Alabama, or the Light Armored Vehicle Repairman Course at Camp Pendleton. EOD marines deploy in ground troops that support aviation and infantry units. Some specialties include:

- Ammunition technicians: These marines receive, store, and distribute ammunition and toxic chemicals.
- Small arms repairer/technicians: These marines inspect and repair all small arms used by marines.
- Explosives ordnance disposal technicians: These highly trained marines can locate bombs, identify how they're constructed, and safely disarm and dispose of them. Part of this specialty involves learning how to use robotics. To be eligible for this job, you must have earned the rank of sergeant.

CELEBRITY MARINES

There is no such thing as an ex-marine. The following famous folk all endured the Crucible before finding fame elsewhere:

NFL running back Michael Anderson, the 2000 Offensive Rookie of the Year, played on the 11th Force Contact Football team at Camp Pendleton. He was recruited by a coach at Mt. San Jacinto Junior College and later played at the University of Utah before being drafted by the Denver Broncos.

"Once a marine, always a marine" rang true for actor and comedian Drew Carey. He kept the buzz cut and Corps-issued black eyeglasses long after he left reserve service. Country singer Josh Gracin was already a marine when he appeared on *American Idol* in 2003. He didn't win the title, but he did earn a recording contract and cut several records while serving his country. Jamaican-born singer Shaggy joined the marines two years after he moved to New York. He cut his first single while stationed at Camp Lejeune. Go Daddy founder Bob Parsons is a Vietnam veteran who received the Combat Action Ribbon, Vietnamese Cross of Gallantry, and the Purple Heart.

Before he was deemed to have the right stuff, astronaut John Glenn served as a Marine Corps fighter pilot. Composer John Philips Souza, the March King, was leader of the U.S. Marine Band from 1880 until 1892. Talk-show host Montel Williams was the first African American marine chosen to attend the Naval Academy Prep School and graduate from the Naval Academy. He served for fifteen years and received numerous commendations.

Perhaps the most recognizable marine is actor and Gunnery Sergeant R. Lee Ermey. Before he voiced the toy soldiers in *Toy Story* and *Toy Story 2*, he served eleven years as a marine, including one-and-a-half tours in Vietnam. Ermey has appeared in television programs, commercials, and nearly forty movies, including *Apocalypse Now*, *The Boys in Company C*, and *Full Metal Jacket*.

TRANSPORTATION

Marines trained to work in motor transport are in charge of maintaining tactical military commercial vehicles, such as Jeeps. They coordinate with distribution management to move resources, people, equipment, and necessary supplies. Motor transport operations can happen on the ground, via amphibious vehicles, or by air. They use 7-ton (6.4-metric-ton) trucks, HMMWVs, tankers, and other vehicles to achieve their missions.

If you're chosen to train in a motor transport specialty, you'll attend either the Automotive Organizational Maintenance Course or the Motor Vehicle Operator Course at Camp Lejeune. Some specialties include:

- Automotive maintenance technicians: These marines inspect and repair all motor transport equipment.
- Vehicle recovery operators: These marines operate wreckers for any vehicle recovery or lifting and towing operations.
- Enlisted jobs include light and heavy vehicle operators, automotive mechanics, logistic vehicle system mechanics, crash/fire/rescue vehicle mechanics, and semitrailer refueler operators.

CHAPTER 8

ENGINEERING, SCIENCE, AND TECHNICAL

Some of the most technologically demanding, hands-on jobs fall under the engineering, science, and technical fields. Advanced weapons, intensive training, and personal readiness will still fall short of accomplishing a mission if communications fail. Marines chosen to serve in the engineering, science, and technical fields serve in the forefront of modern warfare.

Communication is key to success. There are myriad career opportunities in this occupational specialty to analyze and disseminate information. Some of the most clever, responsible, and mature marines will end up in these jobs:

- **Data systems:** Computer whizzes find the perfect job in the data systems field. Marines chosen to train in this field learn computer systems analysis, software design,

This integrated maintenance management systems operator checks the signal of a TRC-170 communication device at Al Asad Air Base in Iraq. The TRC-170 lets marines remain in contact with forces across Iraq.

and computer equipment operation. The main specialty in this field is small computer systems specialist programmer.

- **Drafting, surveying, and mapping:** What would a military force do without maps? How would they have any idea of how the unknown terrain of enemy land falls—the hills, rivers, and rocky outcroppings that can help or hinder a battle plan, or the way a town winds and weaves and creates all kinds of hiding points for both sides of the conflict? Marines chosen for this occupational specialty have exceptional artistic abilities and strong math and logic skills. Some specialties within this field are mapping officers, construction drafters, surveyors, cartographers, and geodetic surveyors.

- **Operational communications:** Marines chosen for this occupational specialty have exceptional technical skills. They design and install communication and information networks to ensure that all forces can communicate. They lay communication wire and install such equipment as computers, cryptographic systems, telephones, and radio. Some of the specialty jobs include field wireman, construction wireman, circuit switch operator, field radio operator, mobile multichannel equipment operator, satellite communications terminal operator, and defense message system specialist.

- **Signals intelligence/ground electronic warfare:** These marines operate the equipment used to collect intelligence, analyze what they find, and communicate the information to others. Some specialties include special communications signals collection operators/analysts and communicator and cryptologic linguists. They work in conjunction with marines in the intelligence field.

- **Intelligence:** Marines chosen for this field collect and process the information collected by the signals intelligence equipment, as well as manual observations and interactions. Marines chosen for this field are among the very best, are adept at communication, are cool under pressure, and have exceptional maturity and people skills. Some of the specialties in this field include counterintelligence, imagery interpretation, geographic intelligence, and interrogator/ translator.

- **Anti-warfare:** The Marine Aircraft Wing requires specialized jobs in air control, air support, anti-air warfare, and air traffic control. Marines chosen to work in this field manage the operation of air command and other functions within the Marine Aircraft Wing. Some marines work in the airfield control tower and radio-radar air traffic control systems. Others serve as navigators, radio and radar operators, and intercept controller anti-air warfare missile batterymen. Occupational specialties include low-altitude air defense gunner, air control electronics operator, tactical air defense controller, air support systems operator, air traffic controller, and radar approach controller.

WEAPONRY

Marines need technical skills to efficiently and correctly manage the weapons used by the Marine Corps. Weaponry-related fields require exceptional technical skills.

Aviation ordnance: This field encompasses aviation ammunition, such as safety, procuring the

A chemical, biological, radiological, and nuclear defense specialist tests suspected nerve agent inside the live nerve agent chamber at the Chemical Defense Training Facility at Fort Leonard Wood.

ammunition, and storing and delivering stock as needed. The main occupational specialty for this field is the aviation ordnance systems technician. Marines trained to serve as these technicians learn how to maintain and repair aircraft armament systems, including gun pods, machine guns, bomb racks, and rocket and missile launcher equipment.

Nuclear, biological, and chemical: Marines in this occupational specialty train to become nuclear, biological, and chemical defense specialists. They learn to detect and identify nuclear, biological, and chemical weaponry. They learn how to decontaminate such attacks on the battlefield and are responsible for warning and reporting to other marines about such attacks.

Ordnance: Marines chosen to train in this field learn to inspect, repair, and maintain most weapon systems. They are responsible for ensuring other marines get the weaponry and materials they need. Some occupational specialties include small arms repairer/technician, towed artillery systems technician, machinist, electro-optical ordnance repairer, assault amphibious vehicle repairer/technician, main battle tank repairer/technician, and light armored vehicle repairer/technician.

Building a Base Camp

Base camps don't just pop up out of nowhere. Marines build these mobile cities from the ground up. They lay pipe and power lines where needed, construct buildings and roads, and create a place where soldiers can do their jobs.

Combat engineers: The marines build and maintain buildings used by the rest of the force. They also demolish sites and operate the Assault Breacher Vehicle for clearing minefields. They complete the basic combat engineer course at Camp Lejeune. Engineer equipment operators learn to operate the equipment used to excavate and grade areas, as well as equipment needed for logging, clearing, and landing operations. The engineer assistant helps prepare architectural and mechanical CAD drawings, and supports planning and management projects.

Construction equipment and shore party: Marines in these fields perform such manual labor as metalworking and welding. They are also trained to operate heavy machinery for construction and clearing space. Specialties include shore party chief, metalworker, engineer equipment mechanic, small watercraft mechanic, and engineer equipment operator.

Utilities: Just like at home, base camps need utilities to function smoothly and create a healthy

SPECIAL FORCES: THE MARINE CORPS FORCES, SPECIAL OPERATIONS COMMAND

You've heard of the Navy SEALs, the Green Berets, the Army Rangers, and the Air Force Special Tactics. You may not have heard about Marine Force Reconnaissance. This team of specially trained forces is not a part of the U.S. Special Operations Command, or USSOCOM, like the other Special Forces are, but Force Recon Marines do carry out reconnaissance missions and complete specific, small-scale military missions that require stealth and skill. Marines in this field receive specialized training and are an elite force of warriors. Force Recon Marines train for several months with the Reconnaissance Training Company at Camp Pendleton.

In 2005, Secretary of Defense Donald Rumsfeld directed the formation of an official special operations group of about 2,500 marines. This group is called Marine Special Operations Command, or MARSOC, and they serve with the USSOCOM. MARSOC candidates train at Camp Lejeune in North Carolina.

Force Reconnaissance companies still exist, and their roles have remained the same. However, there has been some restructuring. The 1st and 2nd Force Reconnaissance Companies transferred to MARSOC

(CONTINUED ON PAGE 98)

SPECIAL FORCES (CONTINUED)

to form the 1st and 2nd Marine Special Operations Battalions, or MSOB. Candidates for the 1st MSOBtrain at Camp Pendleton, while 2nd MSOB candidates train at Camp Lejeune. Each battalion is made up of four Marine Special Operations Companies trained to handle specialized equipment, intelligence missions, and fire support.

To be eligible as an enlisted marine, you must have served for three years or two deployments. Your tryout is intense. You must pass pool and physical fitness tests before you're invited to a three-week screener test. If chosen, you'll endure training conditions even more challenging than boot camp. You'll be tested on mental as well as physical toughness. It takes a special marine to serve in Special Operations or Force Recon.

environment. Marines trained in utilities learn to install and operate water supply lines, electrical lines, plumbing and sewage, and heating and air conditioning. Specialties include electrician, electrical equipment repair, refrigeration mechanic, fabric repair specialist, well driller, and hygiene equipment operator.

Weather service: Weather impacts every aspect of a military operation. Marines need information about conditions on land, in the air, and the ocean. The meteorological and oceanographic

Marines and sailors with the Meteorological and Oceanographic Strike Group team prepare to launch a weather balloon. A transmission system attached to the balloon will send weather data back to the team.

services occupational specialty field is the only earth science–related field in the Marine Corps, and yet it encompasses so much. The only entry-level specialty is METOC observer. To become a METOC analyst, you must either have earned a bachelor's degree in meteorology from an accredited college or complete the Meteorology and Oceanography Analyst/Forecaster Course or the Air Force Weather Apprentice Course at Kessler Air Force Base. You also need top-secret security clearance.

CHAPTER 9

LIFE AFTER THE MILITARY

Any marine will tell you there is no such thing as an ex-marine. But there will come a time when your life as an active-duty marine will end. Your years of service and training will have prepared you for civilian life. Best of all, you'll see benefits unique to members of the military. So what happens after you leave behind the dress blues, the deployment orders, and the barracks?

Easing back into your life as a civilian can be strange or even difficult. You won't be alone. The U.S. Departments of Defense, Labor, and Veterans Affairs offer help in the form of TAP: the Transition Assistance Program. This program will help you navigate the sometimes choppy waters of leaving behind active service. TAP offers financial and legal advice. You can speak with transition counselors. You can get help finding a job. Your family can get help adjusting to suddenly having you around all the time. You can find a TAP office at the Family Support Center on base.

JOINING MARINE CORPS RESERVE

Many people opt to join a reserve branch of the military. They can serve their country part-time while pursuing their education or starting and raising their families. Some reservists serve years without ever seeing active duty, although they realize their commitment means they can be deployed into active duty at any time.

The marines are a bit unique, however. Most marine reservists have already served active duty for at least four years. The common time commitment among marines is eight years—four or six years active and two or four years reserve. The strong connection they build through the months of boot camp and the years of training and missions with their fellow marines is embedded in their bones. They remain marines through and through. Being part of the Marine Corps Reserve lets them continue their training and reaffirm their *Semper Fi* commitment to their fellow marines.

It takes the same stringent requirements to enlist in the Marine Corps Reserve without serving actively

Marine Corp reservists engage in a live training drill at a mock urban village at Camp Pendleton in California. These reservists prepared for deployment to Iraq in summer 2011.

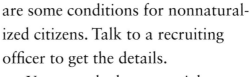

first as it does to enlist for active duty. You must be an American citizen or have a permanent resident alien card, more commonly known as a green card. There

are some conditions for nonnaturalized citizens. Talk to a recruiting officer to get the details.

You must be between eighteen and twenty-eight years old, or seventeen years old with a parent's permission. You must have a high school diploma, although the Marine Corps does consider reserve candidates who have a GED, provided they score well enough on the Armed Services Vocational Aptitude Battery test. Some students join the reserves so that they can train while they attend college. Students who wish to pursue officer positions need to enroll in the Navy Junior Reserve Officers Training Corps. You must pass the same physical fitness test required to enter boot camp. Then you must attend boot camp. Yes, even reservists must attend boot camp, endure the Crucible, and earn the right to be called marine.

EDUCATION ASSISTANCE

We talked about special education allowances active marines can apply for, as well as how some training can equal college credits, thereby shortening your time spent earning an advanced degree. The American Council on Education reviews military training and experiences, and it awards equivalent college credit to service members. More than 2,300 colleges and universities recognize these credits.

Once you leave active service, you are still eligible for tuition help to continue your education. The GI Bill was established in 1944. This government program helped servicemen returning from World War II receive more education or vocational training, as well as help them start businesses or buy homes. The Post-9/11 Veterans Educational Assistance Improvements Act of 2010 builds upon the services first established by the GI Bill.

These changes took place on August 1, 2011. Among the conditions:

Active-duty service members and their spouses using transferred military benefits are eligible for the $1,000 book allowance. At this time, student veterans already receive the allowance.

People taking online or distance courses are eligible to receive living stipends, or money to help offset noneducation costs. Students were required to attend

A marine serving aboard the USS *Kearsarge* studies math equations. Classes are conducted on the ship. These marines gained college credit through Park University while supporting relief operations in Pakistan.

at least one classroom course to qualify before. The payment for online and distance courses is half of the national average living stipend.

Students taking enough courses to be considered at least a half-time student are also eligible for living stipends. Before, only students attending more than half-time could receive stipends.

These changes extend benefits to servicemen seeking nontraditional education, such as certificate and nondegree programs, apprenticeships, and on-the-job training.

The new bill also simplifies the tuition and fee reimbursement cap for private schools, some graduate courses, and for students paying out-of-state tuition. The cap is now set at $17,500 nationwide. This amount is the national average cost of in-state tuition and fees. Before, each state based the cap on the highest public school tuition in the state. The new amount is higher than the previous levels in most states.

Servicemen can use GI Bill benefits multiple times for licensure and certification tests, as well as national college exams. However, students who use the benefit more than once forfeit one month of their thirty-six months of benefits for every $1,667 spent on exam fees.

There are other benefits as well. Veterans between twenty and twenty-four can get free job training and job placement support through the Job Corps program. Job Corps is a program developed by the

Labor Department to train all kinds of young people in growing career fields. There are 123 Job Corps Centers around the country. Veterans get priority placement, but a few centers have reserved three hundred slots strictly for veterans. These centers are in Edinburgh, Indiana; Morganfield, Kentucky; and Excelsior Springs, Missouri. Veterans can get transportation to and from the center. You can also get housing, meals, medical services, career training, a biweekly living allowance, and support with job placement. To enroll, call the VETS/Job Corps project anytime toll-free at (800) 733-5627.

GETTING A JOB

Your time as an active-duty marine will teach you new skills. But as a marine, you'll also bring back a wealth of qualities. You will have a strong work ethic. You will have a sense of integrity and perseverance in your tasks. You will be disciplined and capable of following directions and solving problems.

And there will be employers eager to put you to work because you embody so much of what they want in an employee. The Web site GIJobs.com keeps a list of the top one hundred military-friendly American companies. Check it out when you're ready to go job hunting. For now, here is information on the top five companies that hire former service members:

TRAVEL THE WORLD AGAIN

Marines, like other members of the military, get certain perks, especially regarding travel. Because soldiers must be away from their families and loved ones for so long, all airlines offer what's called Space Available Travel, or "military hops." This means members of the military and their immediate families can fly for free if seats are available. You have to register in advance and wait for a seat to open, but you fly for free.

What's more, you can use these free flights to visit military bases around the world. There are bases in sixteen countries where all service members, regardless of branch, can stay for reduced costs and sightsee off base for fun. You traveled the world to defend America. You can still see the world long after your active service ends, and take your family along with you.

Union Pacific Railroad: This company, headquartered in Omaha, Nebraska, oversees the largest railroad in the United States. Recruiters eagerly seek out military personnel who are returning to civilian life. Why? For the very reasons we already noted: service members have a strong work ethic, solid training, and discipline. The company partners with the Department of Defense TAP program around the country.

CSX Corporation: Another railroad company, CSX is based in Jacksonville, Florida. It also actively seeks out military personnel in transition, especially those with training in logistics, because it knows former service members can forge teamwork in the most demanding work conditions. CSX notes that one in five of its current employees are former military members, and nearly one in four of its new hires is a veteran.

USAA: This insurance and financial services corporation is headquartered in San Antonio, Texas. USAA provides products and services dedicated to helping military service members and their families. Their insurance plans—including auto, home, and life—are designed to meet a family's unique needs and budget.

BNSF Railway: Another railroad and transportation company, BNSF Railway is headquartered in Fort Worth, Texas. BNSF came about after Burlington Northern merged with the Santa Fe Railway. The company seeks out well-rounded candidates with mechanical experience from all military ranks and branches, especially those younger veterans who may not have had the opportunity to earn an advanced degree.

ManTech International Corporation: This defense and electronics manufacturer is based in Fairfax, Virginia. It is among the government's leading providers of technology and solutions for mission-critical

ManTech is one of several American businesses that support veterans looking for work. GIJobs.com is a database of companies like ManTech that actively recruit former service members.

national security programs. Its goods support military intelligence, the Department of Defense, the State Department, Homeland Security, and the Justice Department. The corporation aggressively recruits veterans, citing their technical skills, leadership qualities, and dedication to national security.

Rounding out the top ten military-friendly employers are Johnson Controls (industrial products and services), Norfolk Southern (transportation and logistics), CINTAS (multiple corporate services), Southern Company (energy and utilities), and ITT Corporation (defense and business services).

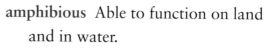

GLOSSARY

amphibious Able to function on land and in water.

Armed Services Vocational Aptitude Battery (ASVAB) The test taken by all military enlistees to determine the training plan.

avionics The science of electronics used in aviation.

battalion A military unit made up of two or more smaller units.

civilian A person who isn't in the military.

close-order drill A marching exercise to practice handling weapons while moving in formation.

company A subdivision of a military regiment or battalion, made up of two or more platoons.

deploy To position troops for combat.

fire team A basic infantry fighting unit of four marines.

gunnery The science of constructing and using heavy guns and projectiles.

IED An improvised explosive device, or homemade bomb.

infantry Marines and other soldiers trained to fight on foot.

insurgent A person who uses force to revolt against a lawful authority.

MOS Military Occupational Specialty.

ordnance Weapons, ammunition, combat vehicles, and equipment used by the military.

platoon A subdivision of troops made up of two or more squads or units.

rappel A controlled slide.

reconnaissance The act of exploring enemy territory to gather information.

sapper A specialized marine combat engineer trained to clear the way by laying bridges, clearing landmines, and so on.

squad A small military group led by a noncommissioned officer.

FOR MORE INFORMATION

Marine Corps Division of Public Affairs

Headquarters Marine Corps

3000 Marine Corps

Pentagon, 4A532

Washington, DC 20350-3000

(703) 614-1034

Web site: http://www.usmc.mil/unit/divpa
The Marine Corps Division of Public Affairs acts as a link between the military and the public. It offers special links for military families, current news, and community relations.

Marine Corps Recruit Training Depot, Eastern Recruiting Region

Douglas Visitors Center

Parris Island, SC 29905

(843) 228-3560

Web site: http://www.mcrdpi.usmc.mil
This depot has been training marines since 1915 and female recruits since 1949. It trains all female enlistees and males who live east of the Mississippi River.

Marine Corps Recruit Training Depot, Eastern Recruiting Region

Parris Island Museum

Parris Island, SC 29905

(843) 228-3560

Web site: http://www.mcrdpi.usmc.mil
This first Marine Corps museum was dedicated in 1975.
The museum helps educate recruits and the public about
Marine Corps history.

Marine Corps Recruit Training Depot, Western Recruiting Region

Command Museum

1600 Henderson Avenue

San Diego, CA 92140

(619) 524-8727

Web site: http://www.mcrdmuseumhistoricalsociety.org
The goal of this museum is to teach recruits and the public alike about the legacy of the Marine Corps. More than
150,000 visitors tour the museum each year.

U.S. Marine Corps Memorial

National Park Service

George Washington Memorial Parkway

Turkey Run Park

McClean, VA 22101

(703) 289-2500

Web site: http://www.nps.gov/gwmp/
marinecorpswarmemorial.htm
The most recognizable image of marines in action—the
raising of the flag at Iwo Jima, February 19,
1945—was captured by World War II photographer Joe
Rosenthal. The four marines were forever immortal-
ized in bronze in 1954. The memorial is dedicated to all

marines who have sacrificed their lives fighting for our country.

U.S. Naval Academy

Visitors Center

52 King George Street

Annapolis, MD 21402

(410) 293-8687

Web site: http://www.usna.edu

The Naval Academy has been training navy and marine officers since 1845. The Visitors Centers welcomes the public and prospective students to view displays that showcase the highlights of American naval science.

U.S. Department of Defense

1400 Defense Pentagon

Washington, DC 20301-1400

(703) 571-3343

Web site: http://www.defense.gov

This government agency is in charge of providing protection through military defense.

U.S. Defense Department Advisory Committee on Women in the Services

Room 2C548A, 4000 Defense Pentagon

Washington, DC 20301-4000

(703) 697-2122

Web site: http://dacowits.defense.gov

The Advisory Committee on Women in the Services is composed of civilian men and women appointed by the Secretary of Defense to provide recommendations on matters and policies relating to the recruitment and retention, treatment, employment, integration, and well-being of highly qualified professional women in the armed forces.

WEB SITES

Due to the changing nature of Internet links, Rosen Publishing has developed an online list of Web sites related to the subject of this book. This site is updated regularly. Please use this link to access the list:

http://www.rosenlinks.com/cod/mari

FOR FURTHER READING

Axelrod, Alan. *Miracle at Belleau Wood: The Birth of the Modern U.S. Marine Corps.* Guilford, CT: Lyons Press, 2010.

Bartlett, Merrill L., and Jack Sweetman. *Leathernecks: An Illustrated History of the United States Marine Corps.* Annapolis, MD: Naval Institute Press, 2008.

Campbell, Donovan. *Joker One: A Marine Platoon's Story of Courage, Leadership, and Brotherhood.* New York, NY: Random House, 2010.

Clark, George B. *Battle History of the United States Marine Corps, 1775–1945.* Jefferson, NC: McFarland, 2010.

Coram, Robert. *Brute: The Life of Victor Krulak, U.S. Marine.* New York, NY: Little, Brown and Company, 2010.

Doedan, Matt. *La Infanteria de Marina de EE.UU./The U.S. Marine Corps.* New York, NY: Capstone Press, 2007.

Dolan, Edward F. *Careers in the U.S. Marine Corps.* New York, NY: Benchmark Books, 2009.

Drury, Bob. *The Last Stand of Fox Company: A True Story of U.S. Marines in Combat.* New York, NY: Grove Press, 2009.

Goldish, Meish, and Fred Pushies. *Marine Corps: Civilian to Marine* (Becoming a Soldier). New York, NY: Bearport Publishing, 2010.

Gray, Wesley. *Embedded: A Marine Corps Adviser Inside the Iraqi Army.* Annapolis, MD: Naval Institute Press, 2009.

Hammel, Eric. *Islands of Hell: The U.S. Marines in the Western Pacific, 1944–1945.* Minneapolis, MN: Zenith Press, 2010.

Haynes, Major General Fred, and James A. Warren. *The Lions of Iwo Jima.* New York, NY: Holt Paperbacks, 2009.

Hearn, Chester G. *Marines: An Illustrated History: The United States Marine Corps from 1775 to the 21st Century.* Minneapolis, MN: Zenith Press, 2007.

Martin, Iain C. *The Greatest U.S. Marine Corps Stories Ever Told: Unforgettable Stories of Courage, Honor, and Sacrifice.* Guilford, CT: Lyons Press, 2007.

Orr, Tamra B. *USMC Reconnaissance Battalions* (Inside Special Operations). New York, NY: Rosen Central, 2008.

Popaditch, Nick. *Once a Marine: An Iraq War Tank Commander's Inspirational Memoir of Combat, Courage and Recovery.* El Dorado Hills, CA: Savas Beatie, 2008.

Roarke, Paul J. *Corps Strength: A Marine Master Gunnery Sergeant's Program for Elite Fitness.* Berkeley, CA: Ulysses Press, 2010.

Smith, Larry. *The Few and the Proud: Marine Corps Drill Instructors in Their Own Words.* New York, NY: W. W. Norton & Company, 2007.

Stein, R. Conrad. *The U.S. Marine Corps and Military Careers.* New York, NY: Enslow Publishers, 2007.

U.S. Marine Corps. *U.S. Marine Guidebook.* New York, NY: Skyhorse Publishing, 2010.

BIBLIOGRAPHY

Benson, Michael. *The U.S. Marine Corps*. Minneapolis, MN: Lerner Publications, 2005.

Bohrer, David. *America's Special Forces: Seals, Green Berets, Rangers, USAF Special Ops, Marine Force Recon*. St. Paul, MN: MBI Publishing, 2002.

Dolen, Edward F. *Careers in the U.S. Marine Corps*. Tarrytown, NY: Marshall Cavendish, 2010.

Halberstadt, Hans. *US Marine Corps (The POWER Series)*. Osceola, WI: Motorbooks International Publishers & Wholesalers, 1993.

Hole, Dorothy. *The Marines and You*. New York, NY: Crestwood House, 1993.

Leckie, Robert. *Helmet for My Pillow: From Paris Island to the Pacific*. New York, NY: Bantam Books, 2010.

Maze, Rick. *"A GI Bill Surprise."* Marine Corps Times.com, December 22, 2010. Retrieved December 30, 2010 (http://

www.marinecorpstimes.com/news/2010/12/
military-gi-bill-surprise-congress-passes-improve-
ments-122210w).

*Military Times Edge. "Job Training Program
Reserves 300 Spots for Vets."* November 30,
2010. Retrieved December 20, 2010 (http://
www.militarytimesedge.com/career/job-hunting/
ed_veterans_jobcorps_120610).

Moses, Corporal. Meloney R. *"Famous Female Firsts:
Turning History into 'Her Story.'"* U.S. Marine
Corps Base Quantico, March 11, 2010. Retrieved
February 1, 2011 (http://www.quantico.usmc.mil/
Sentry/StoryView.aspx?SID=3912).

Palmer, Lance Corporal Charles IV. *"Female Warriors
Earn Place in History."* USMC.com, March 10,
2001. Retrieved February 1, 2011 (http://www.
usmc.mil/unit/mcblejeune/Pages/news/2001/
Female%20warriors%20earn%20place%20
in%20history.aspx).

Payment, Simone. *Frontline Marines: Fighting in
the Marine Combat Arms Units.* New York, NY:
Rosen Publishing, 2007.

The President's Own. *"Resources and References."*
Retrieved January 18, 2011 (http://www.
marineband.usmc.mil/learning_tools/library_
and_archives/resources_and_references/marines_
hymn.htm).

Tomajczyk, S. F. *To Be a U.S. Marine.* St. Paul, MN: Zenith Press, 2004.

USMarineRaiders.com. *"Carlson's Raiders Gung Ho."* Retrieved December 30, 2010 (http://www.usmarineraiders.org/gungho.htm).

USMilitary.com. *"U.S. Marine Corps Jobs— Enlisted Occupations."* Retrieved December 26, 2010 (http://www.usmilitary.com/ us-marine-corps-jobs-enlisted-occupations).

USMilitary.com. *"U.S. Military Officer Job Opportunities."* Retrieved December 26, 2010 (http://www.usmilitary.com/ us-military-officer-job-opportunities).

Willis, Clint, ed. *Semper Fi: Stories of the United States Marines from Boot Camp to Battle.* New York, NY: Thunder Mouth Press, 2003.

INDEX

A

Advanced Individual
    Training (AIT), 30–32
aircraft maintenance
    jobs, 43–44, 46
American Council on
    Education, 104
ammunition and
    explosives ord-
    nance disposal
    jobs, 7, 83–85, 87
Anderson, Michael, 86
Armed Forces Radio
    and Television
    Service (AFRTS), 69
Armed Services
    Vocational
    Aptitude Battery
    (ASVAB), 13, 30, 103
Armour, Vernice, 74
avionics jobs, 51, 52,
    54, 56–57, 71, 85

B

Barnwell, Barbara, 74
base camp, building a,
    96, 98–99
base leadership jobs, 73
Billeb, Bertha, 74
BNSF Railway, 109

Brewer, Margaret, 74
Butler, Smedley, 36

C

Camp Geiger, 30, 38
Camp Lejeune, 31, 46, 79,
    83, 86, 87, 96, 97, 98
Camp Pendleton, 30,
    31, 38, 41, 46, 75,
    85, 86, 97, 98
Carey, Drew, 86
Carlson, Evans F., 20
Combat Action
    Ribbon, 86
commissioned officer,
    becoming a, 16–17
Confidence Courses, 28–29
Crucible, the, 6, 29–30,
    60, 86, 103
CSX Corporation, 109

D

Daly, Daniel, 36–37
data communications
    maintenance jobs,
    51, 59, 61–62
Deal, Sarah, 74
Delayed Entry
    Program (DEP),
    15, 17

deployment, strain of on
   family, 75–78

E

education assistance, 82,
   104, 106–107
electronics maintenance
   jobs, 51, 62–63
Emblem Ceremony, 30
Ermey, R. Lee, 87

F

Family Readiness Program, 75
family support programs,
   75, 77, 101
field artillery jobs, 33–35, 71
Fort Belvoir, 65
Fort Huachuca, 46
Fort Knox, 39
Fort Meade, 65
Fort Sill, 34

G

GI Bill, 104, 106
GIJobs.com, 107
Glenn, John, 86
Gower, Charlotte Day, 70–71
Gracin, Josh, 86
gung ho, meaning of, 20

H

Holcomb, Thomas, 55

I

infantry jobs, 33, 37–38, 45, 85
Initial Strength Test (IST), 19, 21

J

Jobs Corps, 106–107
Johnson, Opha Mae, 70

K

Korean War, 45

L

Lejeune, John, 37
Lentz, Anne, 70
logistics jobs, 79, 81

M

ManTech International
   Corporation, 109, 111
Marine Aircraft Wing, 62, 93
Marine Air Ground Task
   Force (MAGTF), 48, 59
marine careers
   combat specialties, 33–41
   electronic/electrical sys-
      tems, 51–65
   engineering, science, and
      technical, 89–99
   logistics and supply, 79–88
   personnel and base sup-
      port, 66–78
   vehicle/machinery and
      mechanics, 42–50

Marine Corps Exchange, 68, 69
Marine Corps Martial Arts
   Program (MCMAP), 22
Marine Corps Reserve, 9,
   12, 70, 86, 101, 103
Marine Corps Tuition
   Assistance Program, 82
Marine Corps Women's
   Reserve, 70, 71
Marine Force
   Reconnaissance, 97–98
Marine Officer Candidates
   School, 17
Marine-Option
   Midshipman, 16
marine recruiter, questions
   to ask a, 12
marines
   basics, learning the, 18–32
   celebrities, 86–87
   having what it takes, 8–17
   introduction, 4–7
   nicknames, 8, 45
   women, 33, 70, 74
"Marines' Hymn," 55–56
Marine Special Operations
   Battalion (MSOB), 98
Marine Special Operations
   Command (MARSOC), 97
Medal of Honor, 36
military, life after the, 101–111
military-friendly employers,
   107–111
Military Occupational Specialty
   (MOS), 30, 34, 42, 46
Moran, Geraldine, 74

motor maintenance jobs, 46,
   48, 50
Mountain Warfare Training,
   4, 6, 16
Mutter, Carol, 74
"My Rifle," 40

N

Naval Junior Reserve
   Officers' Training Corps
   (NJROTC), 9, 16, 17, 103
Navy and Marine Corps
   Medal, 74

O

Oath of Enlistment, 15
Offenbach, Jacques, 55
Officer Candidate School, 16
Operation Desert Storm, 49

P

Parris Island, 6–7, 18, 38
Parsons, Bob, 86
Physical Conditioning
   Platoon, 21
Post-9/11 Veterans
   Educational Assistance
   Improvements Act, 104
post-traumatic stress disor-
   der (PTSD), 78
Purple Heart, 86

R

Rumsfeld, Donald, 97
Rupertus, William, 40

S

sappers, 41
School of Infantry East, 30, 38
School of Infantry West, 30, 38
security clearance, levels of, 51–52
Semper Fi, 60, 101
Servicemembers Opportunity Colleges, 82
Shaggy, 86
Silent Drill Platoon, 25
Souza, John Philips, 86
Space Available Travel, 108
Special Forces, 97–98
Streeter, Ruth Cheney, 70
supply administration jobs, 82–83

T

tank and armor jobs, 33, 38–39, 41, 49
training and audiovisual support jobs, 51, 65
Transition Assistance Program (TAP), 100–101, 108
transportation jobs, 87–88

U

Union Pacific Railroad, 108

USAA, 109
U.S. Department of Defense, 51, 100, 108, 111
U.S. Department of Homeland Security, 111
U.S. Department of Justice, 111
U.S. Department of Labor, 100, 107
U.S. Department of State, 111
U.S. Department of Veterans Affairs, 100
U.S. Marine Band, 86
U.S. Naval Academy, 16, 87
USS *Dan Daly*, 37
U.S. Special Operations Command (USSOCOM), 97–98

V

Vandegrift, Alexander, 71
Vietnam War, 86, 87

W

weaponry-related jobs, 93, 95
Williams, Montel, 86–87
World War I, 36, 45, 70
World War II, 28, 45, 71, 104

ABOUT THE AUTHOR

Colleen Ryckert Cook is a writer and editor in Kansas City who often writes for children and teens. Her brother trained at MCRB San Diego and was stationed at Marine Corps Air Station Kaneohe Bay in Oahu, Hawaii, for four years. His many six-month floats took him around the world, including to Lebanon during the 1983 suicide-bomber attack on a U.S. Marine Corps barrack in Beirut that killed 220 marines, 18 navy servicemen, and 3 army soldiers.

PHOTO CREDITS

Cover (top) © www.istockphoto.com/Bart Sadowski; cover (bottom left), p. 1 (bottom left), cover (bottom right), p. 1 (bottom right), back cover, pp. 52–53; pp. 23, 34, 58–59, 63, 67, 72–73, 76–77, 80, 84–85, 90–91, 94–95, 99, 105 U.S. Marines; cover (bottom middle), p. 1 (bottom middle), pp. 64–65 Patrick Baz/AFP/Getty Images; pp. 1 (top), 102–103 Sandy Huffaker/Getty Images News/Getty Images; pp. 3, 27 David McNew/Getty Images News/Getty Images; p. 5 Kent Nishimura/Getty Images News/Getty Images; interior graphic (camouflage), pp. 8, 12, 18, 33, 42, 51, 66, 79, 89, 100 Shutterstock; pp. 10, 19 Scott Olson/Getty Images News/Getty Images; pp. 14, 43 Defense Video & Imagery Distribution System; pp. 16, 17, 18, 20, 25, 36, 37, 40, 45, 49, 55, 56, 60, 70, 71, 74, 82, 86, 87, 97, 98, 108, 112, 114 U.S. Navy; p. 31 © AP Images; pp. 39, 47 Stocktrek Images/Getty Images; p. 110 ManTech International Corp.

Designer: Les Kanturek; Editor: Bethany Bryan; Photo Researcher: Marty Levick